'A crisp, forceful call to reflect on the meaning
of disruption; Murphy places her stethoscope
firmly on the chest of the modern media, calls it
to account and reveals an uncertain, uncomfortable,
but enduring heartbeat.'
Julia Baird

The internet has shaken the foundations of life: public and
private lives are wrought by the 24-hour, seven-day-a-week
news cycle that means no one is ever off duty. *On Disruption*
is a report from the coalface of that change: what has
happened, will it keep happening, and is there any way
out of the chaos?

A trek along Asia's 'hippie trail' in 1972 led to Tony and Maureen Wheeler creating travel publisher Lonely Planet, and to the *New York Times* describing Tony as the 'trailblazing patron saint of the world's backpackers and adventure travelers'. Recently Tony has been involved with the Planet Wheeler Foundation's international development work and the creation of Melbourne's Wheeler Centre for Books, Writing and Ideas. He still travels a lot.

Writers in the *On Series*

Tony Wheeler

On Travel

Published in Australia and New Zealand in 2020
by Hachette Australia
(an imprint of Hachette Australia Pty Limited)
Level 17, 207 Kent Street, Sydney NSW 2000
www.hachette.com.au

First published in 2018 by Melbourne University Publishing

10 9 8 7 6 5 4 3 2 1

A catalogue record for this book is available from the National Library of Australia

ISBN: 978 0 7336 4396 5 (paperback)

Original cover concept by Nada Backovic Design
Text design by Alice Graphics
Author photograph by Greg Elms
Typeset by Typeskill
Printed and bound in Australia by McPherson's Printing Group

To Maureen—who else would I travel with?

Distance

Everywhere is walking distance if you have the time.
Steven Wright, comedian and film producer

We are two-thirds of the way across the country when I turn on my pocket GPS and hold it up against the window.

'Tracking Satellites', the screen announces, and little bar graphs bounce up and down as it tries to find the four satellites it needs to tell me where I am. After a few minutes, four bars have turned solid and my GPS confirms exactly what the 747's moving map has been telling me, it even agrees on the ground-speed figure, precisely 882 kilometres per hour.

I click on the nearest destinations and several waypoints, GPS jargon for the locations I entered into the device only a year ago, pop up on the screen. Since we're crossing the country more or less from the south-east to the north-west, we have to intersect the route I took, and I'm looking for the place I named M of J. Sure enough, there it is, only 109 kilometres away, and travelling at 14 kilometres a minute we're getting rapidly closer. At first it seems like we're heading directly towards it, but then it's clear we're going to pass just a little bit to the east. We're at 33 kilometres distance, 32, 31.9, 31.8 and then 31.9 again.

Of course, I am not only 31.9 horizontal kilometres from the Minaret of Jam, I am also 35 000 feet above it, and those 10 vertical kilometres make all the difference in the world. Sitting in my comfortable window seat, a glass of wine on my fold-out table, I could just as easily be 10 000 kilometres from Afghanistan, that gloriously spectacular country unfolding beneath me—mountainous, barren, with rivers tracing streaks of green down the valleys, and scratches of roads winding alongside them and sidling away to climb some mountain pass.

Thirty-five years earlier I'd first encountered that lonely minaret, with its Pisa-like lean, as a travel poster on the wall of a Herat hotel. I'd never heard of the Minaret of Jam, but that one picture was enough. I wanted to go there. A messy revolution, a Russian invasion, the chaotic, greedy, violent squabbles of assorted mujahedin (they were Russia's enemies, so they must be our friends), the arrival of the Taliban and then 9/11 and its various aftermaths delayed my return trip for far too many years, but in the pre-dawn light of a May morning in 2006 my Toyota Hilux rolled out of Herat and headed due east. It felt curiously appropriate that in Afghanistan I was riding in the four-wheel drive regularly cited as the terrorist's vehicle of choice, from Mogadishu to Mazar-e Sharif.

The first 150 kilometres through Obe and Chisht-e Sharif, with its graceful, decayed *gumbad*, were no problem, but then the road deteriorated and the vehicle *Top Gear* rates as near indestructible began to earn its reputation. It was less than 300 kilometres from Herat to the minaret, but the trip took fifteen hours, and we arrived after nightfall. I gratefully unrolled my sleeping bag on the floor of the guesthouse near the minaret, just 32 kilometres from where my 747 would pass over one year later.

Distance, it's what travel is so often about. We may travel great distances, but the reality is that small physical distances can still mean huge separations. Afghanistan may be just 10 kilometres below me, but it's still a world away. Back home I could drive 10 kilometres in less than ten minutes, but in our Airbus or Boeing we fly overhead while poverty, overcrowding, violence, wars see the unnoticed below us.

That gulf of separation has always intrigued me about travel. We can be so near, yet so far, and it isn't only thin air beneath our wings that can separate us. Language can do the job just as well. We could be standing in the same room, breathing the same air, and yet be separated by an unbridgeable gap: we cannot communicate.

Or we cannot understand. Our beliefs, our fears, our concepts are so different that even communication cannot lead to understanding.

We travel for all sorts of reasons. It can be simple escape, a change from the working-week routine, a chance to get away from our problems, to forget everyday life.

Or it can be much more. We may travel in search of beauty. Music, art, writing, nature can all thrill us with their beauty, and so can travel. Who hasn't been left open-mouthed in wonder by the splendour of something seen or experienced 'on the road'?

It can be simply to satisfy an urge, a need to travel. We've been infected by wanderlust and the only way to scratch that itch is to go somewhere. It's been a human condition from the earliest days—isn't going walkabout an Australian term? Today, we have greater opportunities to satisfy that nomadic urge.

It can be the need to make the pulse beat faster, to live life a little on the edge. There is a subcategory of travel where you deliberately seek out the dangerous places; the government travel advisories are an attraction rather than a warning.

And having travelled everywhere, there's the simple pleasure of coming home. Nothing makes home as sweet as being away from it.

Whatever the reasons for travel, it's the thing that puts us in the same room, puts us in contact, helps us to bridge the gap, and to build the understanding that only travel can bring. We do so much of it, we jump on so many planes, sleep in so many hotel rooms, eat so many restaurant meals, that travel and tourism have become the biggest single component of the world's economy. The World Travel & Tourism Council estimates that, including direct and indirect factors, it accounts for nearly 10 per cent of the world's GDP, that one in every twelve jobs on earth is travel related.

Of course, travel has its downside—you don't do so much of anything without doing some damage somewhere—but I firmly believe that, overall, the effects are positive. In so many places, the travel business brings increased prosperity, and usually it's prosperity that brings peace—the world's most unstable places are the most poverty-stricken.

Beauty

*… the most beautiful things I had ever seen
had all been seen from airplanes.*
Joan Didion, journalist and novelist

I've taken Joan Didion's words in *The Year
of Magical Thinking* to heart. I'm unhappy if
I don't score a window seat. Yet rarely, as I
look around the aircraft cabin, is anyone else
looking out the window. I want to yell, 'Look
outside, it's beautiful.'

Or, 'Don't you know what happens down
there?'

I'm flying over the Indonesian island of Java, and off to the west the cone of Mount Bromo pops up through the clouds. From our position, I'd guess it's about 50 kilometres away. A small plume of smoke gently drifts from the top of the volcano.

It's a reminder, yet again, that flying is a miracle and that there's so much to see if we just look. I glance around the cabin to see who else has caught a glimpse of this natural wonder: nobody. Almost every window blind is pulled firmly down, and at the few that are open, nobody is looking.

Often there's nothing much to see; you're flying over the ocean, or it's cloudy down below, or it's just dull, uniform country-side and you're too high up to pick anything out. Other times the view is better than any movie: dramatic mountains (recently, on an Emirates flight from Dubai to Milan, as we tracked just north of the Kurdistan region of Iraq), beautiful islands (deep green against even deeper blue on another flight across Indonesia), endless desert (a flight from Mali to Morocco across the Sahara), endless jungle (Cameroon to the Central African Republic), dramatic cloud formations, or perhaps it's simply another aircraft crossing beneath us, appearing and then disappearing in a flash.

On some flights, if the weather is good, the views are guaranteed to be incredible. It doesn't matter if you're at ground level or 10 kilometres up, Antarctica is always spectacular. There's no subtlety about Antarctica, everything is drama—it's blue or white,

white or black, whether it's snow or ice, sea or sky, penguins or whales. I've been down to Antarctica a couple of times by sea, but I've also flown there on a Qantas 747, a flight to nowhere that started from Melbourne, arrived at the icy continent, flew over it for a spell and then turned around, landing exactly where we had started ten hours earlier. But what a flight.

Fly from London or another northern European city to somewhere down the west coast of North America, like Vancouver, Seattle or San Francisco, and you're almost guaranteed similarly dazzling views. On a flat map it looks like you'll fly straight across the USA, but in fact your flight will arc far north over the Atlantic, across Greenland and Hudson Bay, then track south-west across Northern

Canada, with an Instagram-posting of icebergs and icefloes, then myriad lakes unwinding below you. It's positively magic. So is the early morning approach into Dar es Salaam in Tanzania, when Mount Kilimanjaro, the highest mountain in Africa, just materialises through the dawn clouds.

Any flight across Australia towards Southeast Asia and Europe feels like a combination of a geography and history lesson. From Melbourne, the Murray River is the first sign of a division from the populated fringe to the outback. Then there are those relentlessly parallel sand dunes, followed by endless outback, where at night there always seems to be some isolated fire burning, some lightning-strike-ignited outbreak that will flare up and then burn out without anybody ever seeing it at ground level, a sight reserved for those of us on a passing airliner. Finally, there's that scatter of other-worldly islands off Derby, reminders of William Dampier's early visit as our first whingeing Pom.

Altitude, whether it's gained from a plane or a mountain, can help to crank up the beauty rating, but it's far from necessary. A trip on a shonky, crowded fishing boat, heading from Nukufetau to Vaitupu in Tuvalu, where everyone sleeping on deck is lashed with rain as we pass through a squall, followed by a calm that reveals a vista of stars in a blaze of light across the sky, the Milky Way adding a milk-like sheen. Or standing on a tropical island beach at night, looking across a shallow lagoon to the sliver of white where the sea beats on the outer reef. Views that take your breath away.

There are also mornings when you wake in a tent and peek out under the fly to some incredible view: the Himalayan peaks you didn't have the energy or the time to admire as night fell, the flight of noisy parrots that have woken you on your walk along the Larapinta Trail in Central Australia. In fact, so many views of outback Australia, where there is always a horizon. Standing on an outcrop just north of the Tanami track at sunset and watching a trail of dust behind some dot-of-a-vehicle heading west and, to complete the picture, a mob of kangaroos considerately materialising and bounding off in another direction.

We can impose human order on to nature and it will still be beautiful. The tidy fields that make England such a green and pleasant land. Lines of grapevines marching metronomically across the landscape in a wine-growing region of France. Or the throat-catching beauty of rice fields cascading down a hillside in Bali or China.

Even our cities can be beautiful. The stalagmite-like array of skyscrapers stretching across Manhattan, the convoluted maze of buildings in some Italian hill town, or the even more tightly wound labyrinth of construction in a Moroccan medina. Standing on the fort walls in Jodhpur in India as a gentle ripple of noises drift up from the streets below. The sparkle of lights as a city comes alive at night.

Wanderlust

When you come to a fork in the road, take it.
Yogi Berra, baseball player and cultural icon

Why do Australians travel so much?

Perhaps it's the tyranny of distance—we're a long way from anywhere. Head to Europe from the east coast and you've already been in the air for four or five hours before Derby and the Western Australian coast disappears below you. It comes down to simple economics: by the time you're out of Australia, you might as well stay out for a long spell and travel a lot.

Or it's the cultural cringe: things must be better, more interesting, more exciting over there. Success at home doesn't count, it has to be achieved in London or New York (or these days, Shanghai) for real recognition.

Or it's our convict history: we came here unwillingly, we never wanted to be here, we get away at the first opportunity. The Australian and American settlement experience may be superficially similar—turn up in a new world from the old one, overwhelm the native inhabitants, do very well for yourself—but Americans were fleeing the old world when they turned up, they never had any intention of going back. Even today they don't travel a lot. Far from fleeing, the First Fleet Australians were flung out, exiled against their will, with return uppermost in their minds. No wonder so many of us have passports and travel so much.

Or perhaps it's an even older history that has somehow seeped into our veins. From the earliest encounters, the European observers noted the Aboriginal tendency to down tools and go walkabout for no discernible reason. Perhaps we've simply been infected by something that's always been in the country.

There is that slightly feral nature of the outback as well; our love affair with it is coloured with a hint of caution. One wrong move and the love affair can turn bad, you can be quickly added to the long list of outback casualties. Careless tourists don't merely *die* back of Bourke, they suffer that quintessentially Australian fate, they *perish*.

For whatever reasons, we do travel a lot. Statistically, a large percentage of us have passports, we travel more often, and we spend longer abroad or even on the road in our own country.

Travel is like any other addiction: the more of it you've had, the more of it you need. You risk infection with what Canadian novelist Douglas Coupland defines as 'terminal wanderlust', a condition where nowhere's home, or anywhere could be.

Of course, Australians are far from the only people with a modern version of the old nomadic instinct. The Germans on every scale—as a nation and on a per capita expenditure basis—can probably lay claim to being the world's most active travellers. In typically German fashion they even managed to define and record what it took to be infected. In the 1970s the German Globetrotter Club had a simple membership requirement: make a trip that keeps you on the road for twelve months. Moving somewhere and setting up shop, taking up a foreign posting, didn't count. You had to actually travel for a year. I always thought it was a pretty good measure; even a six-month trip carries a severe risk of terminal wanderlust infection.

Today, going somewhere totally new or doing something truly original is near impossible. Fork out enough money—US$50 million was the most recent ticket price—and you can even spend two weeks on the international space station. All the most important mountains have been climbed, the poles have been reached by every means of travel imaginable, the ocean depths have been plumbed, and we have circumnavigated the world nonstop and solo. If you want something truly original, it's likely to be from Michael Palin's 'Across the Andes by Frog' school of travel adventure. Does it matter? The view from the top is just as good for the thousandth summiteer as for the first.

Everywhere

I haven't been everywhere, but it's on my list.
Susan Sontag, writer and filmmaker

Well before she had been everywhere, Sontag would have been happily welcomed into the Travelers' Century Club circle. Membership qualifications for this Californian organisation are simple: you have to visit 100 countries. Quite what a visit entails is up to you—just transiting the airport is sufficient to add a tick if you want to play fast and loose. Furthermore, the TCC's list goes a long way beyond the 193 member countries of the United Nations—you can tot up Tasmania and Lord Howe Island as well as the Australian mainland if you're intent on putting a tick beside all the 327 names on the club's checklist.

Of course, the UN's list is a fairly shaky reference in its own right. If Frank Zappa's suggestion that you need at least a beer and an airline to qualify for national status holds true, then Taiwan is certainly a country, UN recognition or not. The Mothers of Invention singer added that a football team and nuclear weapons would cement the claim and, who knows, Taiwan may qualify on those two as well.

Then there are quite a few colonies that most of us think of as countries—do we seriously accept that Tahiti and those other palmfringed patches of paradise are just outer suburbs of Paris? And how do you categorise

Antarctica? Okay, there's no government, not much human population and a large ozone deficiency, but we all agree that Antarctica is a whole continent. Surely that should be good enough for something?

In fact, Antarctica is often the last continent for keen travellers to visit, the place you only get around to visiting when you've already been everywhere. It's not yet 200 years since the first human set foot there. That very well-travelled explorer Captain James Cook may not have set foot on the continent, but he did cross the Antarctic Circle and came within about 120 kilometres of the coast in 1773. The first confirmed sighting of the coast did not take place until 1820, and the first human to set foot on the Antarctic mainland probably did so a year later.

Cook may not have been everywhere, but if crossing the circle was sufficient to allow a 'been to Antarctica' tick in the Captain's log-book, then he may well have been the first person to visit every continent. Born in Europe, his early naval service was in North America, he made landings in South America, Africa and Asia during his three great journeys of exploration and, of course, he visited Australia on the first voyage.

Looking back at my travels at the end of 1997 I realised I'd blithely managed the same feat during the course of the past twelve months. I'd started the year in Australia, trav-elled down to Antarctica via South America in February, and during the rest of the year I'd visited Africa, Asia, North America and Europe. Between February and September

I'd been to every continent without even thinking about it; clearly travel has become much easier since the good Captain's day.

I'm ashamed to admit I do keep track of where I've been. The British would define keeping a list of the countries you've been to as a rather 'anorakish' thing to do, although geeks and nerds might do it as well. I'm somewhat purist about it—just touching down at the airport is not enough. (I could add Cameroon, El Salvador and a few other countries to my tally if it was.) I have met several people who have been, by their count, everywhere. One of them did indeed count airport transits and similar shortcuts as good enough to make a claim. Curiously, although I felt his supposed visit to North Korea was very undeserving, I later duplicated his method, for its sheer surreal quality.

I went to North Korea, absolutely the strangest, most unusual place I have ever visited. Like most visitors to North Korea, I made the trip down to the DMZ, the Demilitarized Zone, a typical piece of military doublespeak, where the rather timeworn and ramshackle military might of North Korea faces off against the more modern, if less single-minded, military might of South Korea. The multi-lane but extraordinarily uncrowded Reunification Highway—like the Hume Highway would look if some nuclear apocalypse had depopulated Australia—connects Pyongyang with the DMZ. If unification ever does take place, it would be even less distance to continue south from the DMZ to Seoul.

At the DMZ two imposing buildings face each other across the border, and between them, actually straddling the borderline, are three nondescript blue-painted wooden huts. Meetings between North Korean and South Korean officials take place in these huts, sitting around a table that also straddles the border. We were duly escorted into the middle one of the three buildings. We entered through the door from North Korea and once inside we were faced with the other door, guarded by two North Korean soldiers, which led to South Korea. Like Alice in Wonderland's rabbit hole, the doors led into utterly different realities. Inside the hut we could casually stroll around the table—North Korea, South Korea, South Korea, North Korea.

For that undeserving North Korea visitor—an English gentleman who was definitely an anorak—visiting North Korea had been purely a matter of entering from that door and walking round to the North Korean side of the table. His travels took him no further into the north. As soon as I saw the southern door I knew I wanted to go through it as well. So, a year later I took a bus tour from Seoul and came into the same wooden hut. This time, a single South Korean soldier blocked the matching door into the north, standing there in an exaggerated martial-arts-style posture. The sheer absurdity of the exercise delighted me. The two doors into the building were only 15 metres or so apart, but to exit from the northern one and then to enter from the southern would require driving back 120 kilometres to Pyongyang, flying 800 kilometres to Beijing (I'd come to Pyongyang from Beijing by train), flying another 950 kilometres to Seoul, and finally taking the 60-kilometre bus ride to the southern door.

Speed

I travel not to go anywhere, but to go.
I travel for travel's sake. The great affair is
to move.
Robert Louis Stevenson, novelist and
travel writer

I made one flight on a Concorde and halfway across the Atlantic realised that I was not only travelling through the upper atmosphere at twice the speed of sound, I was also travelling back through time. In those halcyon pre-9/11 days, a polite request would usually lead to an invite to go up front to watch the flight crew at work. The Concorde flight deck was prehistoric, more like that of a World War II Lancaster bomber than the computer-screened 'glass cockpit' of a modern aircraft. This was ancient technology, the captain and copilot seated in front of row upon row of dials and switches, instead of the digital readouts they would have been facing in a newer aircraft.

I'd preceded my few hours of supersonic flight with a week of travelling at a much slower speed. I like walking. I like to think that on foot you're seeing the world at the pace God intended, and some years back I made a promise to myself that I'd try to do at least one long walk a year. 'Long' meant at least a week, and that morning I checked in at Heathrow straight from Bath, where I'd arrived after a week or so walking along the Cotswold Way from near Stratford-upon-Avon.

Clearly, God has a variety of views on how fast and in what direction we should see the world. It took me four days to circle Mount Kailash, the mountain that is holy not only to Tibetan Buddhists but also to Hindus, who revere the peak as the home of Lord Shiva, and to Jains and to followers of Bön, the pre-Buddhist Tibetan religion. The followers of Bön walk their mountain circuit anticlock-wise, while other walkers travel clockwise. Tibetan Buddhists usually complete their 52-kilometre *kora* in one solid day's walk-ing, including the climb to the 5600-metre Drolma La, a heady 270 metres higher than the Everest Base Camp. That is, if they're not spending three weeks prostrating themselves around the mountain, a process that involves stretching yourself out full length on the ground, then standing up, placing your heels where your fingertips had reached and repeating the procedure.

I only bothered with lying full length at the four designated *chaktsal gang* or 'prostration points'. Even if you don't do it the hard way, completion of a *kora* not only elevates your fitness levels, it has the additional benefit of wiping out your lifetime's sins. This lifetime, that is. More circuits are required if you want to clean up other lifetimes; 108 circuits are required for the all-lifetimes clean-up job.

There are many other religious reasons to walk. Christian walkers like to follow the Way of St James, the Camino de Santiago, which leads to the Spanish town of Santiago de Compostela, where, if you've managed to walk at least 100 kilometres and have enough stamps in your pilgrim passport, you can claim to be a real pilgrim. If you're Japanese, then the *henro*, the 88-temple circuit of the island of Shikoku is the pilgrimage of choice. For Hindus, there's the trek to the Amarnath Cave in the Indian state of Jammu and Kashmir to see Shiva's ice *lingam*. Unfortunately, the *Hajj*, the Muslim pilgrimage to Mecca, is only open to followers of Islam.

Of course, there's no need for a religious incentive to enjoy walking. If some of the most beautiful things I have seen have been from aircraft, plenty more of them have been from ground level, and I've had to walk to get there. I've stood on a hill above Grasmere in

England's Lake District and appreciated why Wordsworth tended to wander in a lonely fashion around there. The view is utterly different, but following the magnificent Larapinta Trail along Central Australia's MacDonnell Ranges can be equally inspiring.

Does arrival by plane ever have the same feeling of achievement, of bagging a hard-won prize, that arriving at surface level can give you? I've returned to Kathmandu by plane many times over the years, but it was that original feeling coming over the edge of the valley, dropping down to a town that, at the time, felt like Shangri-La, which has always stayed with me. It was all the train and bus trips that led across Asia and, finally, up into the Himalayan foothills that made that arrival so important.

Of course, outright speed is not the complete ticket to today's increased speed of travel. It wasn't the Concorde that raced more people to more places more often, it was Southwest Airlines, easyJet, Ryanair, Jetstar and the other 'low cost carriers' that convinced us to rush off somewhere for the weekend because it was so much cheaper than staying at home and going out.

Today, many of us travel further and faster simply because it's so easy and so cheap. Why drive or take a train or bus when you can fly for less? And why do it only once in a while if you can afford to do it every weekend? In Britain, the question 'Where should we go for a weekend break?' means where in Europe, or even further afield. The tourist business of many second-level European cities has become totally dependent on the operational whims of easyJet or Ryanair.

Fortunately, like slow food, slow travel is also becoming a viable alternative. We may pause in our travels to improve our culinary skills or to study Spanish in Guatemala, French on the Côte d'Azur, Indonesian in Ubud or indulge in any of a host of other educational opportunities. Seeing everything at breakneck pace may seem like a young person's pursuit—Europe in twenty-one days with Contiki—but in fact young people are equally liable to kick back, hang loose and watch the weeks drift past.

Home

No one realizes how beautiful it is to travel until he comes home and rests his head on his old, familiar pillow.

Lin Yutang, writer and philosopher

'Holiday home' has to be a modern oxymoron—a holiday is something we do when we leave home, isn't it? Yet some of the very best travel doesn't involve much travel at all, it's simply going somewhere and putting down temporary roots. If the travel experience improves when we slow down, then surely the best travel of all is the slowest of all, simply going somewhere and going native? Certainly some of the best—and bestselling—travel books are about that attempt to establish another home, perhaps somewhere comfortably familiar, but with a better climate and more interesting food. Even dealing with the builders—who display all the same undesirable habits as the ones back home—is more interesting when it's done in French, Italian or Indonesian.

Or there's the attempt to make a home somewhere utterly, scarily different from the familiar one—an Antarctic exile at one extreme, a tropical castaway at the other. Two of my favourite travel tales encompass exactly those extremes. In 1961, Duncan Carse was dropped off with 12 tons of supplies on a remote beach on the island of

South Georgia to enjoy a spell as an Antarctic Robinson Crusoe. Three months later a freak wave washed Carse, fast asleep at the time, his hut and most of his supplies into the sea. Remarkably, he managed to crawl ashore and salvage enough equipment to survive the frigid winter until a passing sealing ship rescued him four months later. Perhaps even more remarkably, Carse, in an earlier incarnation, was the voice of special agent Dick Barton in an enormously popular BBC radio serial, which ran for over 700 episodes from 1946 to 1951.

Tom Neale was a much more traditional castaway, spending sixteen years in three separate spells on the out-of-the-way island of Suwarrow in the Cook Islands. His book *An Island to Oneself* has made his island a pilgrimage spot for Pacific yachties. Tom Hanks also made an island into a pilgrimage spot with the movie *Castaway*. In the film, his far-flung island is fleetingly revealed as somewhere south of the Cook Islands; in reality, it's Monuruki in the tourist-heavy Fijian Mamanuca group. Pilgrimages to Monuruki are much easier than to Suwarrow.

Even as castaways, we seem to want the comforts of home. Weather apart, Carse was doing okay until the unexpected wave swept his supplies away. Island life for Tom Neale was much more organised than for Tom Hanks. Like Carse, Neale wasn't shipwrecked, his castaway spell was carefully planned and well provisioned. We're fascinated by Robinson Crusoe in part because he managed to turn his isolated hideaway into a reasonable facsimile of home. For would-be pilgrims, the island that inspired Daniel Defoe's tale is off the coast of Chile, and it's possibly the ultimate indicator of the power of tourism that the Chileans have renamed it Robinson Crusoe Island.

The things that make home so comfortable and familiar are often exactly what we're trying to cast off when we travel. The pleasure of a tent is that it's not home; it may have few of the comforts of home, but it also contains few of the responsibilities. So long as you've taken the 'travel light' lesson to heart, the zen of travel is exactly that—it can be a zen existence, stripped back to essentials.

Sometimes we simply need to leave home, to get kicked out of that comfortable nest, just like fledgling birds. Certainly, some of the young gap-year travellers, the offspring of British friends, who arrived on our door-step tended to look slightly shell-shocked, exactly as if they'd fallen out of a comfortable nest. I strongly approve of that British invention; the 'gap year' between school and further education usually means travel, and very often to the Antipodes. Tertiary education after a spell in the real world is inevitably a far better experience than immediately following school. I reckon a good gap year of travel provides far more education than the last five years of school.

Damage

Comfort has its place, but it seems rude to visit another country dressed as if you've come to mow its lawns.

David Sedaris, humorist and writer

Travel is never harmless. Overall, I believe the positives outweigh the negatives, whether it's for us personally (we come back tanned, relaxed and, hopefully, a little wiser) or for those we've visited (hopefully we've left them a little wealthier and possibly a little wiser as well). Unfortunately, that education and wealth transfer undoubtedly has some costs attached to it; there's ugly tourist development as well as ugly tourists. Sometimes there's nothing worse than sitting next to the development without being involved with it, suffering the drawbacks without enjoying the benefits.

I'm not too worried about the idea that some locations are in danger of being loved to death. Barcelona and Amsterdam have complained recently that they're 'over touristed'. Venice is another visitor favourite that's long been cited as being at risk. But Venice can look after itself. It's too bad if it's been turned into a real-life Disneyland, but if tourists weren't keeping it alive, the Italians certainly wouldn't. Irrespective of Robert Benchley's famous telegram 'Streets full of water. Please advise', nobody really wants to live long term in a flooded city.

Dubai, on the other hand—now there's a real-life Disneyland with some big question marks hanging over it. If you were going to build a bunch of artificial islands just a metre or two above sea level, and you had heard somewhere that increased carbon dioxide output could lead to global warming and rising sea levels, would you work even harder at pumping out more of it? Does burning energy to artificially cool the hot beach sand for visitors' tender feet or building an indoor ski slope when the temperature outside is usually 40 degrees–plus sound like a good idea?

Today's concern is that we're not just going to love certain destinations to death—low-lying ones could easily end up underwater anyway—but that we'll knock off the whole planet. Of course, there are lots of contributing factors to global warming, but our habit of incessantly going places will certainly hasten the rapidly rising carbon dioxide levels, and thereby help to melt the ice caps, raise the global air temperature and wreck everything.

Air travel may not yet be the biggest contributor to global carbon dioxide output—the airline industry likes to claim that it's only 2 per cent or so of the total—but it's certainly growing rapidly. Aircraft may continually improve their efficiency with more seats, better aerodynamics, less thirsty engines and lighter construction, but a 10 per cent improvement is no help when there are also 20 per cent more wings in the sky. Looking out the terminal window at all the aircraft parked at their gates, or pondering how many more aircraft lined up ahead have to get into the air before it's your turn on the runway will show you just how pervasive air travel has become. For a truly frightening illustration of the sheer size of the airline business, you only need to call up the Flightradar24 app on your smartphone screen, swipe side to side and up and down and you can see every single airliner currently in the sky somewhere in the world.

If we're not worrying about contributing to global disaster, we're fretting about how we impact fragile cultures. We loudmouthed tourists corrupt everything with our demands that food should be just like what we get at home, that we should be provided with all the comforts of home, that the natives speak English, that we have ready access to our media on our tablet and on TV, that our mobile phones roam and the internet connections are always online. Not to mention that with or without tourism, global ubiquity is going to overcome us all. We're all going to end up wearing Nike shoes, eating Big Macs, driving Toyotas, and listening to Taylor Swift and Ed Sheeran on Spotify.

But just how fragile are those local cultures? The Balinese may ride their motorcycles and scan their smartphones, but they'll still turn up for traditional dance practices and gamelan rehearsals. France may get 80 million tourists a year—more than any other country on earth, although China is scheduled to overtake that figure before long—but does anybody believe that French culture isn't as strong as ever?

Well, if we're not devastating the local culture, we're exploiting it. We turn the locals into barstaff, waiters and room cleaners. We turf the fisherfolk off the beach so we can recline on the loungers at our tourist-only beach enclaves and work on our suntans. Village water supplies are diverted so that swimming pools can be filled for visitors at all-inclusive resorts, luxury hideaways where everything is imported and local products never get a look-in. Even when we go trekking in the mountains we recruit the locals to carry our baggage for peanut wages, and don't bother to ensure they're adequately clothed when we drag them up to altitudes they'd never normally encounter.

The cruise-ship business can be a particularly unpleasant side of mass tourism. The mega-cruise ships that sail out of Miami more frequently than interstate trains pull out of Southern Cross Railway Station bargain with the nations of the West Indies for the honour of hosting them. Keep those landing fees down or we'll head to the next Caribbean island down the chain. *Why hassle and haggle with shopping ashore when you can relax at our onboard boutique*, is the message on too many cruise ships. It was undoubtedly apocryphal, but on a visit to Haiti I was told that passengers on the cruise ships that pulled in to a fenced-off beach zone at Labadee were informed that they were landing for the day at 'Paradise Island'—nobody would want to think they were coming ashore in dangerous Haiti. They hardly were: no passports were stamped. Officially, they'd never stepped outside their little foreign enclave.

If, on the other hand, you want a defence of travel, look at the world's wildlife. An

African elephant would be just a big, grey crop-trampler if it wasn't for the tourists it can attract. Perhaps scuba divers are all that stand between sharks and shark fin soup. Unfortunately for the sharks, there may be too many nouveau riche Chinese gourmets keen to knock a bowl of fins back, and not enough scuba divers to protect them.

Costa Rica has developed an economy almost totally centred around not just tourism but a particular form of tourism. Over the last thirty years, Costa Rica has tossed aside agriculture and forestry to concentrate on becoming the world's poster ad for the merits of ecotourism. Although there are places there that feel like a grown-up's, real-world version of Disneyland, you still get the feeling that Tasmania could take some lessons from Costa

Rica. Perhaps we could send some Tasmanian woodchoppers and their government supporters there on holiday?

Sometimes tourism can pull you out of the fire when nothing else is working. With the Soviets footing the bill, Fidel Castro could afford to turn his back on tourism, only opening his beaches to a handful of holiday-makers from behind the Iron Curtain. 'Warsaw with palm trees, but without Solidarity,' was one description of Havana in the years when it looked like Communism might still have worked. When it no longer worked, Fidel quickly decided that tourism might not be such a bad thing after all. That is, if he could farm the nasty money-making side of it out to Spanish capitalists, who'd learnt how to run a beach resort along the Spanish Costas. That way, the Cuban Communist party could take its financial cut, but the general Cuban population wouldn't have to dirty their hands by turning a profit. In his later years, Fidel began to loosen up a touch, and little brother Raúl took it even further, but there are still plenty of owners of *paladares* (private restaurants) and *casas particulares* (private accommodation) who are hoping that Miguel Díaz-Canel will extend it even more.

Money

When preparing to travel, lay out all your clothes and all your money. Then take half the clothes and twice the money.

Susan Heller, writer and traveller

We take so much money when we travel, that by many measures, travel, tourism and all their associated activities have become the biggest single driver of the world's economy. Almost any country counts tourism as an important component of the national economy. Australia attracts close to 10 million overseas visitors a year who spend about A$40 billion, a contribution of about 4 per cent of our GDP, a fairly typical First World figure. For some developing-world countries, however, tourism is more than just a useful contribution, it's *the* major contribution. In Nepal, for example, life pretty much comes down to subsistence farming or tourism. Himalayan trekking is a major part of the Nepalese economy.

You quickly pick up on whether a place is safe or unsafe when you travel there, and it's equally evident how a place works economically. We've seen the figures, we've donated to the charities, we know assorted countries in Africa are penniless, stumbling from one disaster, one civil war, one famine, to the next, but that's nothing compared to visiting the African nation and actually feeling how close things are to the economic edge. I'd never been to a place like Ethiopia, which felt so thin, so worn, so close to the precipice, although after my trip there, more experienced Ethiopian visitors suggested it can look different after the rains. Elegantly impoverished is how the Ethiopian people looked to me, like a Third World version of some threadbare English aristocracy down on their luck, still keeping a stiff upper lip, but wondering how they're going to pay the bills next week. Despite which, Ethiopia is some distance from the bottom of the African per capita wealth figures, and in recent years the economy has improved dramatically.

Or Haiti—it's the poorest country in the Western Hemisphere; if it was in Africa it would be down towards the bottom of that continent's list. That's evident from the first drive into town; this is a country where everybody has to hustle to make ends meet. But in Haiti it isn't the people who tell the tale so much as the country itself. Ethiopia might be overpopulated and the countryside can look stressed—a place where a tree would be worried, and have a right to be worried—but Haiti is on a whole other level. Want a definition of deforestation? Take a look at Haiti.

It's easy to see that Haiti or assorted other countries are poor, and it's equally easy to pick up that a country is well off. Or simply doing better. Returning to Istanbul for the first time in a decade, I found the cars shinier, newer, the streets tidier and cleaner, the shops and their displays glossier. Even on the eastern side of the Bosphorus, in the Asian part of this continent-straddling city, my first thought was that this was no longer an Asian city, it had become a European one, and that feeling continued all the way across the country.

A country may have a healthy per capita GNP figure, but it can be surprisingly easy to discover that the wealth is not spread evenly. Just take the wrong exit off a freeway in some big US city or ride a Greyhound bus into town—it's an American joke that Greyhound unerringly chose locations for their bus stations that would eventually become ground zero for impoverishment and dysfunction. Or get off at the wrong subway station, climb up to the street and instantly feel you should have stayed below ground level. Then compare your glimpse of the other side of this advanced, wealthy First World country with places you've been in the developing world. Would you trade life in a developing-world village where, despite the figures, things seem to work, for life in the slums or in project housing in a US rust-belt city?

In many countries, wealth may be spread unevenly, but in some places it doesn't get spread at all. There are plenty of countries where having some extraordinarily valuable natural resource is a curse rather than a blessing. Has oil made Nigeria a better country for its citizens? Or does the money simply go into the pockets of a minority and fuel their corruption? Are pollution and price inflation all the general population get from oil wealth? For many Nigerians, life would probably be much better if oil had never been discovered, and that truth is easy for any visitor to the country to see. Similarly, in recent years the world's largest oil reserves have not saved Venezuela's citizens from destitution.

As far as 'bad' countries are concerned, I've sometimes felt that Mercedes-Benzes are a giveaway. A country dependent on foreign aid to feed its population, but where government officials drive around in shiny new Mercedes, is a bad country. In East Africa they're the *wabenzi*, a Swahili word coined to describe people who can afford to own them. For years I became so fed up with seeing glossy new Mercedes in Africa that I couldn't imagine owning one myself. A convoy of them hurtling through some African capital, travelling far too fast, accompanied by wailing sirens, is even worse.

Mobutu, the long-term ruler of Zaire (now back to being called Congo again), was keen to hurtle around at much more than the speed of a Mercedes, although doubtless he had a few of them as well. His country became steadily poorer throughout his thirty-two years of complete control, but when Mobutu wanted to pop over to Paris for a chat with François Mitterrand, over to New York to address the UN (presumably about economic management and democracy), to Nice to check on his French chateau, to Hong Kong en route to Japan for Emperor Hirohito's funeral or, on one occasion, just take the quick 4000-kilometre trip to Dakar in nearby Senegal, he would simply charter a Concorde from Air France. He had built a long-enough runway at his palace in the jungle at Gbadolite. Could Mobutu have simply flown on a regular Air France flight from Kinshasa, the Zaire capital? Certainly. Could Air France have said, 'We don't think you should be wasting your bankrupt country's money on chartering a Concorde?' Certainly, they were government-owned at the time.

Concordes may be gone now but they certainly aren't the only type of aircraft that tell a tale. Go to an airport where there's a disproportionate number of those heavy Russian cargo aircraft, leavened only by a handful of unmarked private jets. You know something's up.

Travel brings you face to face with this reality. It's one thing to read about bank-rupt African nations crippled by kleptocratic rulers with big-man mentalities, and another to stand toeing the kerbside and eating dust as a fleet of Benzes career by in close formation.

Travelling almost anywhere brings home to you what works and what doesn't. Jokes about Suharto's wife being 'Madame Tien Per Cent' may have had the ring of truth, but it was easy to see that even when the wealthy and connected skimmed off their 10 per cent, Indonesia still worked far better than Nigeria, where the wealthy and connected tended to skim off all 100 per cent. There may be plenty of poverty in Indonesia, but there's far less than there was thirty or forty years ago.

It's instructive to compare countries where victimhood is used to explain everything. There are African nations where today's chaos is blamed on yesterday's colonial history. Meanwhile, there are countries like Vietnam where even serial spells of colonial damage— French, followed by American, followed by some decidedly bad Russian economic advice— have all been stored in history's filing cabinet while the Vietnamese get on with life. Perhaps competing victimhood can be even worse: the suffering of the Holocaust excusing everything on the Israeli side, while the suffering of the Nakba excuses everything on the Palestinian one. When does a statute of limitations finally kick in?

Understanding

*To travel is to discover that everyone is
wrong about other countries.*
Aldous Huxley, novelist and philosopher

In the end, it's why we travel: to understand. Our petty prejudices and certainties get left behind, just like the extra clothes we couldn't stuff into the already overweight bag. The French aren't snooty and unfriendly, we discover after we've had a spell in France and learnt to always say 'Bonjour Monsieur/ Madame' before asking for the morning *quotidien* or baguette. Or we confirm that the

Italians are indeed disorganised and noisy—
but also fun-loving and stylish.

We find that some things are far bigger, far
more *real* in real life, in reality, than they can
ever be in any other situation. A lion on your
television screen or at a zoo is a pale imitation
of the creature that pads by your tent at night
when you're on a safari. In the Masai Mara
in Kenya I could have sworn an elephant
was pulling grass out from right underneath
our tent. In fact, it was probably a hundred
metres away, but it certainly felt like it was
breathing in my ear.

Travel makes connections. It's regularly
pointed out how we opened our hearts and our
wallets to the victims of the 2004 Indian Ocean
tsunami—we knew those people, those places.
As wealthy Western visitors, we'd stayed there,

we'd interacted with them, even if it was only buying a drink at a bar, a postcard on the beach. Or take the opposite situation, the 2017 Myanmar genocide, when villages were burnt, women raped and children murdered, as half a million Rohingya Muslims were pushed across the border into Bangladesh. Few foreigners had visited the Rakhine area of western Myanmar and, after long years of military control in the country, Aung San Suu Kyi was regarded as something close to a saint who could not be criticised. Couple this with our own refugee fears in Australia, and the unfortunate Rohingya were never going to get the same level of support from us.

Travel makes us question accepted truths. Travel around a drug-producing country like Colombia and you're regularly reminded that it's very much a two-way trade. In the 1980s the country's president Belisario Betancur commented to an American journalist that 'we would not have these problems if you were not such excellent clients'. In fact, the drug war in Colombia is, like similar drug wars in other locations, a wonderful example of one group funding both sides of the battle. American taxpayers fund the 'war on drugs', American consumers fund the drug lords, while in the middle the arms dealers do very well out of supplying both sides. With so many people making so much money legally and illegally, it's hardly surprising no government wants to face up to the only real solution to the drugs business: legalise it.

Afghanistan is another country where the drug business contaminates everything and converts a difficult problem into an intractable one. In the 1960s and 1970s, a golden time in the memories of many older Afghanis, the country enjoyed a modest tourist flow. It could be a tourist destination once again if peace ever returns, a situation that could happen much faster if the drug business wasn't financing the Taliban and making the Western forces in the country unpopular when they try to stamp out a farmer's most profitable crop. If we ever legalised heroin we could simply shift Helmand poppy production to Tasmania, where they already grow plenty of those pretty red flowers for legal medical use.

Travel can be a very political act. For years Americans were not supposed to visit Cuba. Unless they were journalists or had some other government-approved reason for dropping in on that den of Communist iniquity just 400 kilometres south of Miami, they could, technically, be fined up to a quarter of a million dollars and face ten years in jail. Under Obama that restriction started to be loosened up, but unfortunately Trump has put the brakes on again. Making a visit to Cuba, as tens of thousands of Americans do every year, continues to be a political act.

Smaller numbers of Americans make the much longer trek to Iran, where they're usually pleasantly surprised at the friendly reception they receive. Yet once again this is a country where, for Americans, a visit is definitely a political statement. By American or Australian standards, Iran's democracy is a poor excuse for the name, but line up the countries between India and Europe, and until you get to Turkey or Israel, it's about the best on offer. It's certainly way ahead of Saudi Arabia, which continues to be an absolute nonstarter in that field.

Fortunately, as Australians we don't have countries that our government actually forbids us to visit. But there are plenty of places the Australian government advises us we should not be going unless we really have to. There's no question that a prime reason for establishing an immigration detention facility on the island of Nauru was because it is very difficult to travel there and is thus well away from public and media attention. Alexander Downer, Australia's foreign minister at the time the detention centre was opened, commented in 2008 that Nauru was one of the two worst places he had ever had to go—the low-lying Pacific island of Kiribati was the other.

There are places where you're familiar with their history—you know the backstory—but somehow, actually being there has an impact that gets beneath the skin in a way that only visiting can. When I read Anne Frank's diary I was a teenager, much the same age as the diarist, and yet it was not until I actually visited that Amsterdam attic hideaway a decade later that the impact of her story was really driven home. Any reminder of her—most recently a statue in, of all places, San José in Costa Rica—still brings tears to my eyes.

We know on paper Poland's tragic history: the Allies launched into World War II because of Germany's invasion, but at the end of the war the country was handed over to the

Russians. The Warsaw Uprising Museum makes it abundantly clear what the Poles went through towards the end of the war, when the Russians not only casually stood to one side as the Germans brutally put down the uprising, but also stood in the way of the Americans and British offering any help. The result was both the almost total destruction of Warsaw and the annihilation of Poles who might have opposed the Russian takeover. Once again, reading about it is one thing, seeing what happened, where it happened, is an entirely different and more moving proposition.

Travel inland from touristy Dubrovnik on the Croatian coast to Mostar in Bosnia-Herzegovina, where the Mostar bridge was also a bridge between Christians and Muslims, until it was brought down by Croatian artillery

in 1993. Today you can stand on the recon-
structed bridge and gaze at the gigantic cross
on the hill overlooking the city. It's said to be
sited at the point where the artillery did their
work, and pointedly towers above the city's
minarets.

Memphis has Graceland and Sun Studio,
but it also has the Lorraine Motel. Today it's
the National Civil Rights Museum, where the
story of the fight against segregation winds
its way through a series of exhibits in the gut-
ted and rebuilt old motel to finally emerge
in room 306, from which the 39-year-old
Martin Luther King stepped to his death on
the room's balcony, shot by a racist sniper on
4 April 1968. As you make your way through
the museum, you ride the segregated bus, sit
in the segregated diner, imbibe the storyline

of what it was like to be black in the USA in that era, and then emerge into that ill-fated room. No civil rights textbook is going to bring that story home as powerfully.

A final thought

I travel a lot; I hate having my life disrupted by routine.
Caskie Stinnett, travel writer and editor

That's a good enough excuse for me. Soon after I get back from one trip, I'm developing itchy feet and making plans for the next.

We travel for all sorts of reasons, and that travel brings good and bad results. In recent years we've seen a falling birthrate and a slowing in the rate of population increase across many of the world's countries. We've come to realise that in the developing world, smaller families may lead to greater affluence, but in fact it's a virtuous circle that often requires the affluence to come first. Smaller families don't lead to greater affluence, it's greater affluence that leads to smaller families. Then that lower birthrate loops around to yet greater affluence.

Tourism and travel may directly damage the environment, but they can also bring increased affluence in their wake, which can lead to a lower rate of population increase and, in turn, less pressure on the environment. Does one balance the other? I don't know, but look at a country like Kenya, which had the world's highest birthrate not too long ago. Kenya has experienced a dramatic fall in birthrate and it's a country where tourism plays an important part in the economy. In

1970 in Kenya, the total fertility rate—the number of babies a woman had—was eight; a half-century later it's down to four. The story is even more dramatic in Iran. At the time of the Iranian Revolution in 1979, when the Shah departed and the Ayatollah Khomeini ushered in all that ancient Islam, the total fertility rate was also around eight. Today it's similar to that of the most advanced countries in Europe and Asia, jiggling along just under the replacement level of 2.1.

If there's a single cause of political instability in our world, it's the fact that there are too many people—particularly young males—combined with not enough work. The wealth tourism brings can play an important part in mitigating both sides of that problem.

As visitors we not only learn, we also witness, and for many countries the tourist witness has become increasingly important. When everyone carries a mobile phone and every mobile phone is a camera, it's become very difficult for anybody to hide anything. When there are visitors around, there can be fewer dirty secrets. We see and experience things, we learn and understand, we can bring wealth and employment, and there's absolutely no better way of encountering the kindness of strangers. Travel certainly disrupts my routine.

Read
'On'

Little Books,
Big Ideas

'A superbly stylish and valuable
little book on this century's great
vanishing commodity.'
Annabel Crabb

Acclaimed journalist Leigh Sales has her doubts, and
thinks you should, too. Her classic personal essay
carries a message about the value of truth, scrutiny and
accountability—a much-needed, pocket-sized antidote
to fake news.

Donald Trump, the post-truth world and the instability
of Australian politics are all examined in this fresh take
on her prescient essay on the media and political trends
that define our times.

Sarah
Ferguson
On
Mother

'An elegantly written, deeply personal story
of a daughter's grief after her mother's sudden
and mysterious death, with a true-crime
investigation at its heart.'
Jennifer Byrne

A mother's love over decades and across continents.
The sudden death of Sarah's mother reveals their
relationship with poignant clarity and shows her the
individual who existed beyond motherhood. A reflection
on mothers and daughters.

'A crisp, forceful call to reflect on the meaning
of disruption; Murphy places her stethoscope
firmly on the chest of the modern media, calls it
to account and reveals an uncertain, uncomfortable,
but enduring heartbeat.'
Julia Baird

The internet has shaken the foundations of life: public and
private lives are wrought by the 24-hour, seven-day-a-week
news cycle that means no one is ever off duty. *On Disruption*
is a report from the coalface of that change: what has
happened, will it keep happening, and is there any way
out of the chaos?